To Lynne

with love from

Christine

x

"For in the dew of little things the heart finds its morning and is refreshed"

The Prophet

Christmas 2001

SERENITY

SERENITY

To find
serenity,
call a truce
with the clock

Armand Charnay, *The Park of Sanae*

When I walk
I part the air
and always
the air moves in
to fill the spaces
where my body's been.

from *Keeping Things Whole*, Mark Strand

7

I part the air

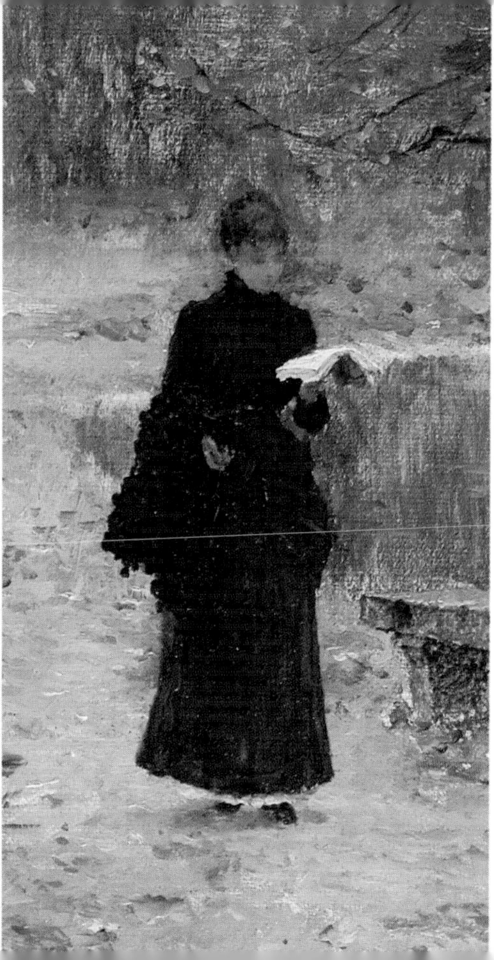

Pierre-Cécile Puvis de Chavannes, *Summer*

Our children swim like river otters
and as their laughter reaches us,
    we join them for a while
in these hottest of summer days.

from *Within Seasons*, Peter Blue Cloud

12

# of summer days

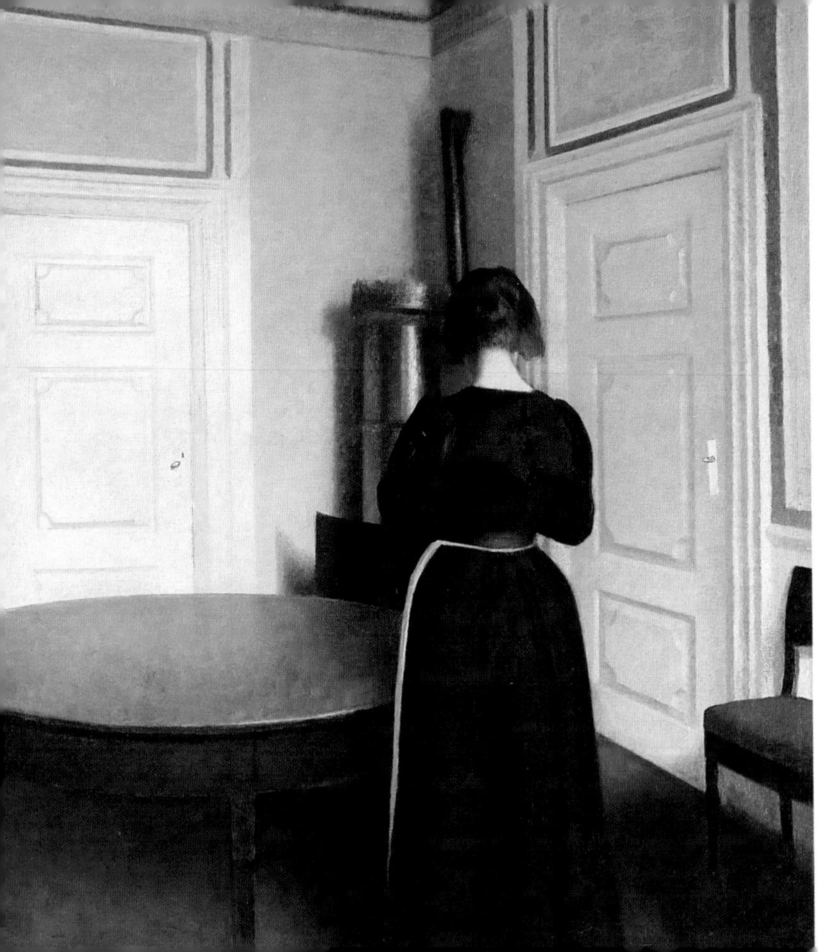

Vilhelm Hammershoi, *Interior*

I'll close all windows and shutters

And build my magic palace in the darkness   15

from *Landscape*, Charles Baudelaire

close all windows

Jules-Louis Dupré, *Willows, with a Man Fishing*

Here dwell in safety,
Here dwell alone,
With a clear stream
And a mossy stone.

from *Spring Quiet*, Christina Rossetti

Here, dwell alone

It is so small
a thing to have
enjoyed the sun

from *Empedocles on Etna*,
Mathew Arnold

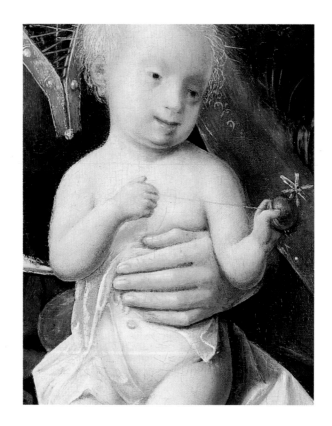

so small a thing

Jean-Baptiste-Camille Corot, *Cows in a Marshy Landscape*

Silent cattle stare
        with green eyes.
They mosey in evening
        calm down to the water.
And the lake holds its
        immense spoon up to
        all their mouths.

from *Dusk in the Country*, Harry Edmund Martinson

silent cattle stare

The joys of marriage are the heaven on earth,
Life's paradise, great princess, the soul's quiet,
Sinews of concord, earthly immortality,
Eternity of pleasures; no restoratives
Like to a constant woman.

from *The Lady's Trial*, John Ford

31

joys of marriage

The gravid mares
graze out their months in gentle stateliness,
freed from all human burdens by their own,
kept close in care, pastured in shady fields
where quiet rivers lap the quieter moss
that lines their banks.

from *The Georgics*, Virgil

in gentle stateliness

36

One flower at a time,
I want to hear what
it is saying

from *Bouquets*, Robert Francis

One

flower

at

a

time

Eugène Boudin, *The Beach at Tourgeville-les-Sablons*

To stand by the
sea or walk again
along a river's
bank and talk with
a companion, to
halt watching
where the edge of
water meets and
lies upon the
unmoving shore.

from *An Elegy for D. H. Lawrence*,
William Carlos Williams

the edge of water

Imitator of Giorgione, *Nymphs and Children in a Landscape with Shepherds*

And when you lie down, your bodies will take beautiful sinuous curves, relaxed as if on clouds

from *A Class in Greek Poise*,
Ruth Draper

sinuous curves

Happy the man, whose wish and care

A few paternal acres bound,

Content to breathe his native air

  In his own ground.

from *Solitude*, Alexander Pope

A few paternal acres

I saw Eternity the other night,

Like a Ring of pure and endless light,

All calm, as it was bright

from *The World*, Henry Vaughan

Geertgen tot Sint Jans, *The Nativity, at Night*

endless light

To gaze at the river made of time and water
And recall that time itself is another river

from *Ars Poetica*, Jorge Luis Borges

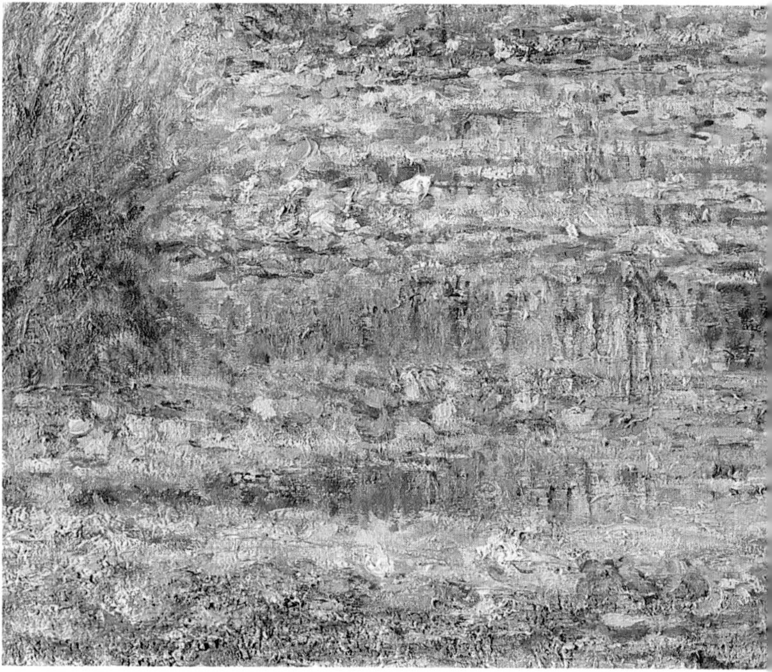

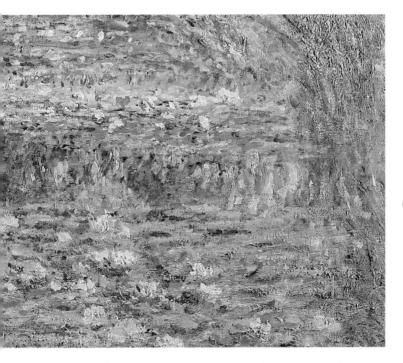

time and water

Trailing silver, shelled in music
    Through this flowering frontispiece.

from *June*, Medbh McGuckian

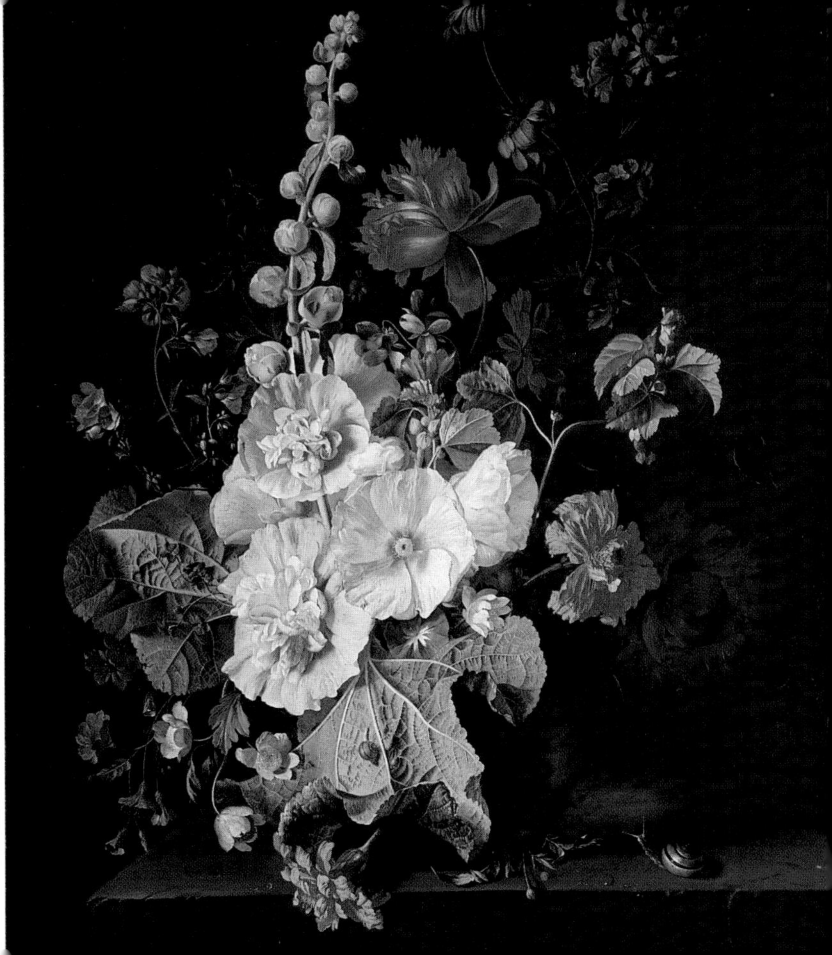

Jan van Huysum, *Hollyhocks and Other Flowers in a Vase*

shelled in music

It is a beauteous evening, calm
   and free;
The holy time is quiet as a nun
Breathless with adoration

from *Evening on the Beach*, William Wordsworth

Jean-Baptiste-Camille Corot, *Evening on the Lake*

calm and free

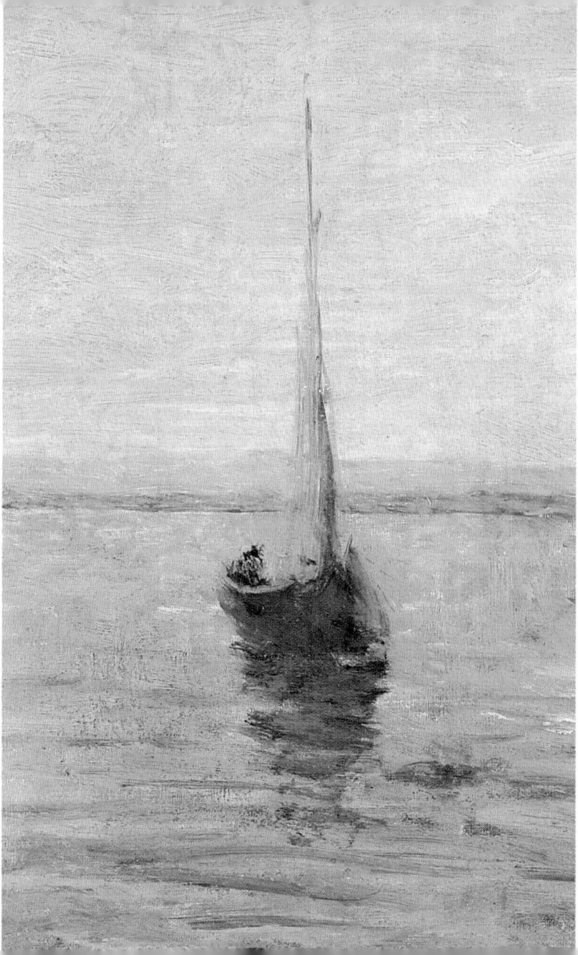

sitting comfortably

And pluck till time and
    times are done
The silver apples of
    the moon
The golden apples of
    the sun.

from *The Song of the Wandering Aengus*, W. B. Yeats

Claude, *A Seaport*

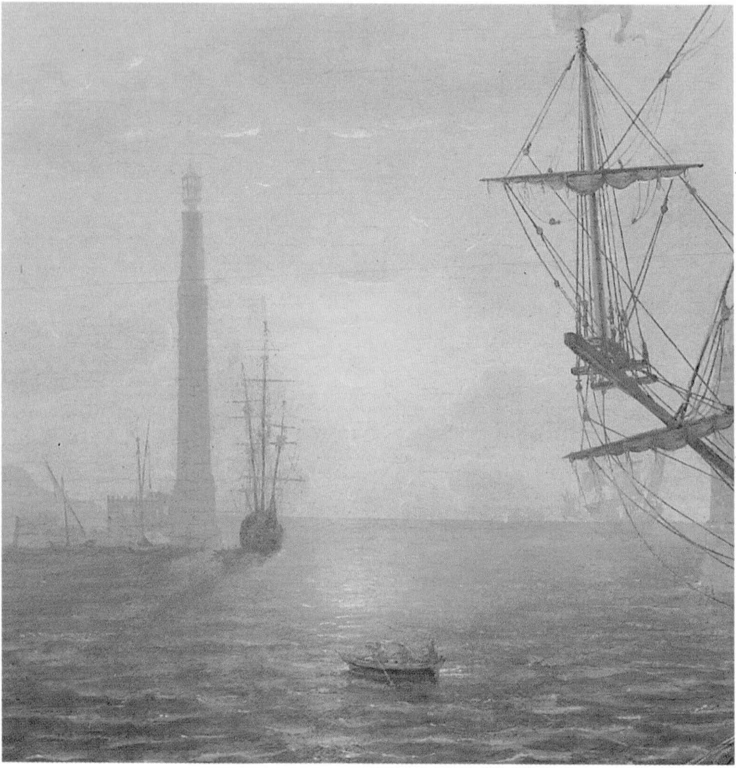

76

golden apples
of the sun

You tell me that silence is

nearer to peace than poems

from *Gift*, Leonard Cohen

nearer
to
peace

More dear art thou, O fair and fragile blossom;
    Dearest when most thy tender traits express
The image of thy mother's loveliness.

from *To Ianthe*, Percy Bysshe Shelley

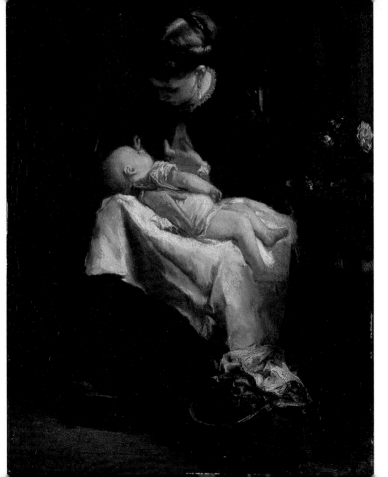

83

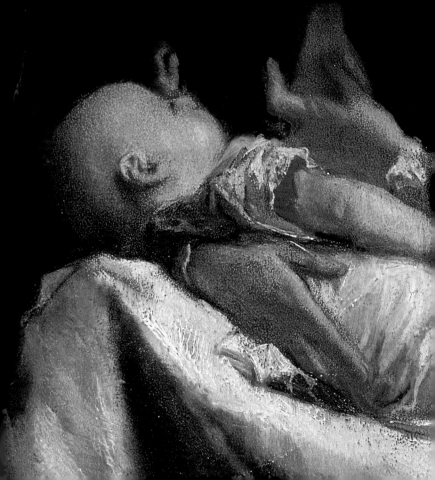

I was born upon thy bank, river
　　My blood flows in thy stream,
And thou meanderest forever
　　At the bottom of my dream.

from *I was Born upon thy Bank, River*, Henry David Thoreau

in thy stream

Rembrandt, *An Elderly Man as Saint Paul*

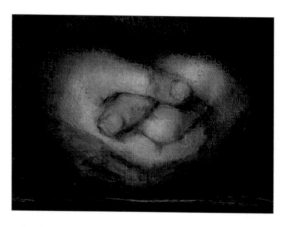

Now I am old

The rivers and their
flowered lawns; the
gleaming birds: and
their song – I heard
that clear I know.

from *The Garden*, Harold Monro

Jean-Désiré-Gustave Courbet, *Young Ladies on the Bank of the Seine*

I heard that clear
I know

97

I stand and wonder how
So zestfully thou canst sing?

from *The Blinded Bird*, Thomas Hardy

Vincenzo Catena, *Saint Jerome in his Study*

... take down this book,

And slowly read, and

dream of the soft look

Your eyes had once,

and of their shadows deep

from *When You are Old*, W. B. Yeats

And slowly read

To make a prairie it takes
    clover and one bee, –
One clover, and a bee,
And revery,
The revery alone will do
If bees are few.

To Make a Prairie, Emily Dickinson

revery
alone
will do

ACKNOWLEDGEMENTS

The editor and publisher gratefully acknowledge permission to reprint the copyright material below. Every effort has been made to contact the original copyright holders of material used. In the case of any accidental infringements, concerned parties are asked to contact the publisher.
*Bouquet*s, reprinted from Robert Francis' *Robert Francis: Collected Poems, 1936–1976*. (Amherst: University of Massachusetts Press, 1976) Copyright © 1936 by Robert Francis.

An Elegy for D. H. Lawrence by William Carlos Williams. from *Collected Poems: 1909–1939, Volume 1*. Copyright © 1938 by new Directions Publishing Corp., Reprinted by permission of New Direction Publishing Corp.
Ars Poetica, from *Dreamtigers* by Jorge Luis Borges, translated by Mildred Boyer and Harold Morland, Copyright © 1964, renewed 1992. By permission of the University of Texas Press.

June by Medbh McGuckian published by the Gallery Press. © Medbh McGuckian.
Extract from *When You Are Old* by WB Yeats by permission of AP Watt Ltd on behalf of Michael B Yeats.
Gift, © 1999 Leonard Cohen. Used by Permission/All Rights Reserved.
Winter Paradise by Kathleen Raine from *Selected Poems* used by permission of Lindisfarne Books, Hudson, NY12534.

110

INDEX OF PAINTINGS

Published by MQ Publications Ltd.
254–258 Goswell Road, London EC1V 7RL
in association with National Gallery Company Ltd.

Copyright © MQ Publications, Ltd.,1999

Series Editor: Ljiljana Ortolja-Baird
Designer: Bet Ayer

A CIP catalogue record for this book is available
from the British Library

ISBN: 1 84072 132 4

Printed in Italy